"What A Deal!
The Louisiana Purchase

by Carole Marsh

Editor: Jenny Corsey

Cover Design: Victoria DeJoy

Design & Layout:
Cecil Anderson
Lynette Rowe

©Carole Marsh/Gallopade International/Peachtree City, GA
©2003 Paperback ISBN: 978-0-635-02123-6
©2010 Library Binding ISBN: 978-0-635-07532-1

Published by

GALLOPADE™
INTERNATIONAL

800-536-2GET
www.gallopade.com

CAROLE
MARSH
BOOKS

Gallopade is proud to be a member of these educational organizations and associations:

The National School Supply and Equipment Association
The National Council for the Social Studies

1

Other Carole Marsh Books

Lewis & Clark Go On a Hike: The Story of the Corps of Discovery
Orville & Wilbur Wright . . . Step Out Into The Sky!

State Stuff™, available for all 50 states:

My First Pocket Guide
State My First Book
State Wheel of Fortune Gamebook
State Survivor Gamebook
State Illustrated Timelines
"Jography!": A Fun Run Through Our State

The State Coloring Book
The Big Reproducible Activity Book
State Millionaire Gamebook
State Project Books
Jeopardy: Answers & Questions About
    Our State

1,000 Readers™

Louisiana Purchase
Thomas Jefferson
The Wright Brothers
Samuel de Champlain
Medard Groseillieres
Juan Ponce de Leon
Christoper Newport

Lewis & Clark
James Monroe
John Cabot
Christopher Columbus
Louis Jolliet
Father Jacques Marquette
Jean Nicolet

Sacagawea
Marquis de Lafayette
Jacques Cartier
Francisco de Coronado
Robert de La Salle
René Ménard
Nicolas Perrot

Patriotic Favorites™

Patriotic Favorites Coloring Book
Star Spangled Banner Activity Pack
My American Flag Activity Pack

Young Patriots Coloring & Activity Book
America the Beautiful Activity Pack
The Pledge of Allegiance Activity Pack

2

Table of Contents

A Word From the Author.. page 4

The Year Was 1803... page 5

What A Deal! The Louisiana Purchase................................ pages 6-7

Setting the Stage.. page 8

Brave St. Domingue Slaves!... page 9

Help!... page 10

The French Connection.. page 11

Peaceful Purchase... page 12

Around the Globe.. page 13

Don't You Agree?.. page 14

Build A Raft!.. page 15

A Growing Nation.. page 16

Rollin' On The River... pages 17-18

Mississippi Mud Pie.. page 19

The Important Visitor.. page 20

Different Folks... page 21

Sail Away!... page 22

Crops, Goods, Services, and Citizens................................. page 23

Just Imagine.. page 24

Add Unto U.S.. page 25

Louisiana Purchase Trivia... page 26

Urgent Telegraph!!!.. page 27

Pen A Poem... page 28

Celebrate the Louisiana Purchase Bicentennial!..................... page 29

Additional Resources to Explore!...................................... page 30

Glossary.. page 31

Answer Key & Index.. page 32

A Word From the Author

What would you do if some kid offered to sell you a really awesome bike for just $2.00? You'd sit back and think, "I know that bike is worth several times that amount!" You also might think about how you could really use that bike to ride home after school. Why would that kid want to sell you the bike for so little? Maybe he needs the cash right away. Maybe he has other bikes. Regardless, the deal is smack dab in your face. Right this moment. Take it or leave it!

Two Americans faced that same kind of situation in 1803. And they managed to make the right decision—one that changed America in a BIG WAY!

In the early 1800s, the United States was still a very young country (they had only just declared independence 1776!). Powerful, older countries controlled all the land around their borders. The Americans were not nervous or scared, but they did want to protect their country from danger. France controlled a lot of land west of the U.S. border, so President Thomas Jefferson wanted to find out what they planned to do with it. He sent a guy named Robert Livingston (kind of like the U.S. ambassador to France) on a secret mission to find out.

Then the situation turned upside down and started moving fast! The port of New Orleans (in the Louisiana Territory) was unexpectedly closed to all Americans. Jefferson quickly sent James Monroe (a future U.S. president) to help Robert buy the city of New Orleans. While they were collecting their thoughts, Napoleon Bonaparte surprised them with an offer to sell the entire territory! He regretted the offer as he made it, but Napoleon had no other choice (as you will see!).

Those two were stuck with a big decision. And there was no email connection to send a message back home for advice! They knew this was the deal of a lifetime. They also knew this would mean going way over what they were allowed to spend (by more than $10 million!). But they knew that if America bought this land, we would be all be a lot safer. They knew our nation would grow. So they took a risk. And we did grow—into one of the most successful countries on the planet!

Carole Marsh
From the Louisiana Purchase
bargaining table
June, 2003

The Year Was 1803 . . .

 January
President Thomas Jefferson sends James Monroe to France. Congress says he can spend $2 million to buy New Orleans and the Floridas. He and Robert Livingston start bargaining.

 March
French dictator Napoleon Bonaparte wants to expand his empire in the West, and Spain secretly transfers Louisiana to France.

 April
Napoleon tells Foreign Minister Charles Maurice de Talleyrand to offer all of Louisiana to the United States. France and American negotiators finally agree on $15 million for the property.

 May
Treaties are signed to seal the deal!

 July
The United States finally receives news of the Louisiana Purchase on July 3!

 October
The U.S. Senate ratifies the treaty, even though some say the constitution does not allow the president to make a land purchase.

 December
On December 20, Louisiana is officially transferred to the United States!

5

"What A Deal!"
The Louisiana Purchase

Thomas Jefferson

Napoleon Bonaparte

When James Monroe and Robert Livingston went to France to buy New Orleans, they had no idea what they would end up bringing home to America. They were sure in for a big surprise! They bargained for a city, but French dictator Napoleon Bonaparte offered the whole shebang!

The $15 million dollar price tag on the Louisiana Territory worked out to about four cents per acre. Can you imagine what that land costs today? Wow! That's why some people have called the 1803 Louisiana Purchase the greatest real estate deal in history!

Setting the Stage

Napoleon Bonaparte took control of France in 1799. At the time, France controlled land in the West Indies and the Mississippi Valley so Napoleon began thinking of how he could expand the French empire and his own power.

Napoleon was a powerful dictator who was known for his military victories. What is a dictator? What kind of government does a dictator rule under? Sort of none! He IS the government.

There are two basic types of government: limited and unlimited. Limited government includes a constitution that makes sure no one person has too much power. It ensures that the people have a say in what happens. In a limited government, everybody has to obey the laws. The rights of individuals are also protected under this system.

Unlimited governments are either authoritarian or totalitarian. Authoritarian means one person or very small group gets all the power, like a dictator. Totalitarian government controls every part of the people's lives. In both situations, the people do not have a voice, have little or no privacy, and often cannot keep government leaders from gaining too much power.

Read the characteristics below. Mark each one with an L for limited government or a U for unlimited government.

_____ Elections and voting rights

_____ Religious freedom

_____ No privacy from the government

_____ People help regulate the power.

_____ Free trade and business

_____ Cannot disagree with the government

_____ No freedom of the press

_____ Freedom to own and sell property

_____ One person has all the power.

BALLOT BOX

8

Brave St. Domingue Slaves!

After the Seven Years' War ended in 1762, France had to give a large portion of Louisiana to Spain. Now Napoleon wanted it back. So the king of Spain agreed to secretly exchange Louisiana for a kingdom in Italy for his brother-in-law. A rare peace was established between France and Britain in 1801, so Britain gave back two islands, Guadeloupe and Martinique, to France.

Napoleon's goal was to connect these two islands, which lay south of North America, to Louisiana with trade routes so that France would grow richer and more powerful. His plan almost worked. But some ambitious slaves changed everything!

The other island that Napoleon needed to control was St. Domingue (Haiti). A brave slave named Toussaint L'Ouverture led the black slaves in a revolt. Napoleon sent his soldiers to stop them, but they were eventually defeated by the slaves and yellow fever. Now he didn't have enough soldiers left to defend Louisiana.

Use an atlas and the Word Bank to identify these countries in the West Indies.

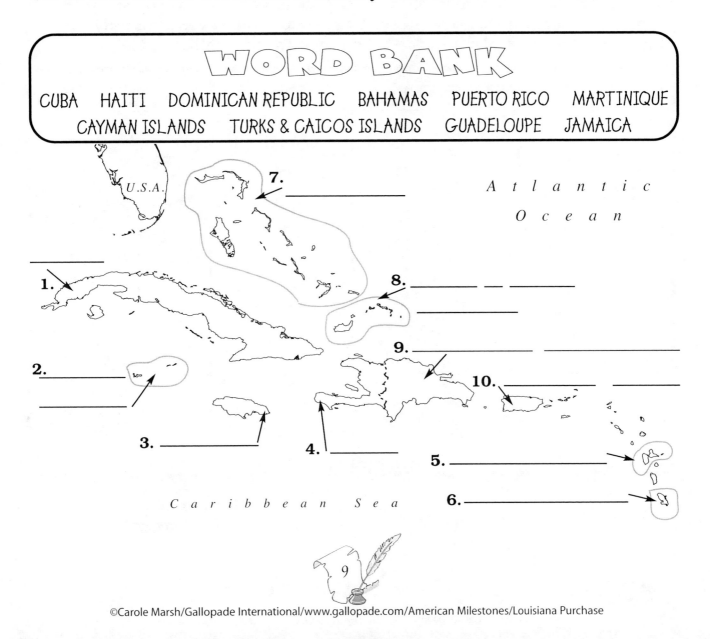

WORD BANK

CUBA   HAITI   DOMINICAN REPUBLIC   BAHAMAS   PUERTO RICO   MARTINIQUE
CAYMAN ISLANDS   TURKS & CAICOS ISLANDS   GUADELOUPE   JAMAICA

U.S.A.

Atlantic Ocean

7. _____

8. ____ ___ __ ____

1. _____

9. _____ _____

2. _____ _____

10. _____ _____

3. _____

4. _____

5. _____

6. _____

Caribbean Sea

9

Help!

Now Napoleon was in a tight spot. He didn't control the island of St. Domingue anymore. Spain wouldn't give up the Floridas region, and Louisiana would be tough to defend without it. Also the British were about to go to war with France again so he needed money to fund the military.

When Spain secretly sold Louisiana to France, Spain still controlled the region. On October 18, a Spanish city administrator closed the New Orleans port to all U.S. shipping. Since 1795, Americans could freely travel up and down the Mississippi River for business. Now they could no longer use the docks and warehouses for their ships and goods in New Orleans.

This action surprised everyone, including Napoleon, and it made the United States very angry! Now that everybody was upset with France, Napoleon decided he would have to change his master plan.

Work out the math problems below to see how export and import taxes can make trade more expensive. Add a 5% tax on all goods. First multiply the original cost by .05 and then add that amount to the original cost.

Item	Original Cost	Tax	Cost After Tax
Blanket	$4.00	$0.20	$4.20
Dress	$2.00		
Hammer	$1.50		
Bushel of Cotton	$3.00		
Nails	$1.00		
Sugar	$1.75		
Flour	$1.25		

Hmmm! Look at that inflation!

Hint: Round your numbers up!

10

The French Connection

On April 11, 1803 Napoleon finally cracked! He called his minister of the public treasury, François Barbé-Marbois, and told him to start talking numbers with Robert Livingston and James Monroe. Barbé-Marbois was a friend to many Americans because he had served with the French military in the United States.

> "I renounce Louisiana. It is not only New Orleans that I cede; it is the whole colony without reserve. I renounce it with the greatest regret; to attempt obstinately to retain it would be folly." – Napoleon Bonaparte (April 11, 1803)

So why did Napoleon ultimately decide to sell ALL of Louisiana to the United States? This territory was larger than Great Britain, France, Germany, Italy, Spain and Portugal combined! There are several reasons, all relating to one common answer: Napoleon had bigger fish to fry!

- *The St. Domingue slave rebellion had left thousands of his soldiers dead, and so his trade plan was out.*

- *At the time, Russia was a threat and enemies were trying to overthrow him, so Napoleon needed all of his resources (money and soldiers) at home in France.*

- *Napoleon did not have enough military power to keep England from invading Louisiana, and he definitely didn't want the British to have a huge western empire in the New World.*

- *If an overseas colonial empire was unlikely, then Napoleon thought that Louisiana was useless to France.*

- *Rather than let the British have Louisiana, Napoleon decided to offer it all to the United States. This way France would also have a loyal ally in the West.*

- *The sale price of $15 million would go a long way toward helping Napoleon build his army back up again and maintain power.*

> "Every eye in the U.S. is now fixed on this affair of Louisiana. Perhaps nothing since the Revolutionary War has produced more uneasy sensations through the body of the nation." - Thomas Jefferson in a letter to Robert Livingston, 1802

11

Peaceful Purchase

When France sold the Louisiana Territory to the United States, a major transfer of land and power took place *without any war*! During those days (and even today), that was a pretty amazing accomplishment.

Many people wish there would be no more wars, but there will always be conflict and disagreement between nations. However, there are many ways to avoid war or even to engage in a shorter war. The Louisiana Purchase negotiations are a great example of how nations can work together to achieve common goals.

Below is a list of ways to deal with conflict. Check those you think would be a good way to avoid war.

_____ Hold peace talks among national leaders.

_____ Bomb enemy cities.

_____ Ask the United Nations to help.

_____ Make fun of the people from an enemy nation.

_____ Send diplomats to smooth things over.

_____ Organize a surprise attack to fix things quickly.

_____ Agree to disagree on minor issues.

_____ Enforce economic sanctions (rules against buying or selling) to make a dictator give up some power.

Fast Fact
New Orleans, Louisiana was an important city. The Battle of New Orleans, the last conflict in the War of 1812, occurred after the war had ended because Andrew Jackson and his army hadn't received the news yet!

12

Around the Globe

There were several countries involved with the Louisiana Purchase, either directly or indirectly. The countries that bordered the United States watched carefully to see how power and land would eventually shift. Actually, everyone was watching. The world powers wanted to see how this potential conflict would end in the New World. The Louisiana Purchase not only increased America's size but helped to shape world history.

Write the name of the correct country in each box.

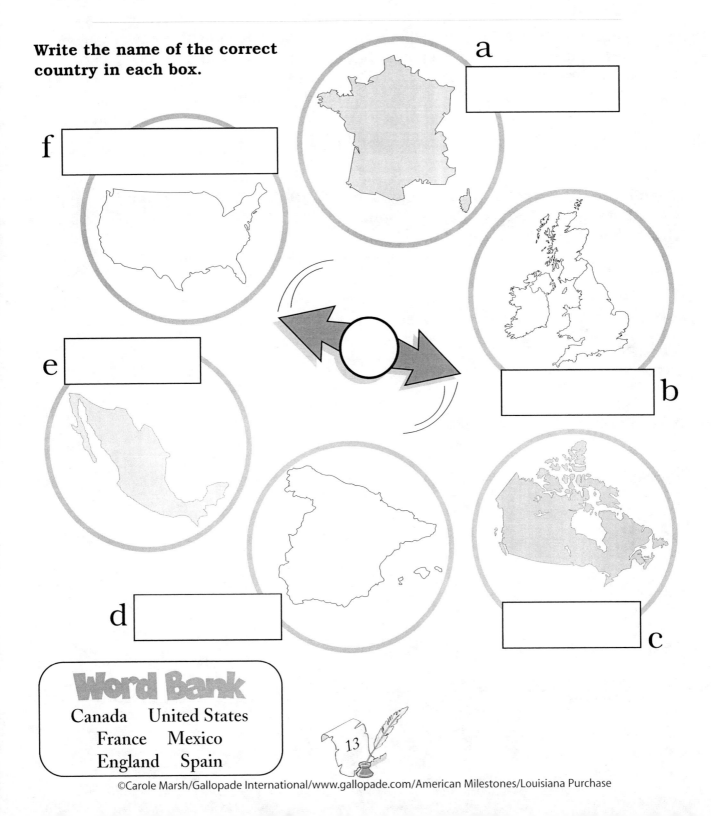

Word Bank

Canada   United States
France   Mexico
England   Spain

13

Don't You Agree?

Not everyone agreed with the purchase of Louisiana. The Federalists, the opposing political party, argued that the U.S. Constitution did not give the president the power to purchase land for the nation. They were right.

However, President Thomas Jefferson thought the purchase was necessary for national security and expansion. He didn't want a powerful country to own land so close to American borders. He decided to do what he thought was best for America. In July of 1803, General Horatio Gates congratulated Jefferson on his actions when he said "Let the Land rejoice, for you have bought Louisiana for a Song."

Regardless of everybody's opinion back home, James Monroe and Robert Livingston were pretty much on their own in France. They ultimately had to make the BIG DECISION. When Napoleon made his offer on April 11, there were no telephones or fax machines to get America's opinion. Monroe and Livingston had to use their best judgement. They took the plunge!

Should America have purchased Louisiana in 1803? Write your opinion below in a paragraph or less. State your opinion and at least two reasons why you think that way.

Build A Raft!

In the 1800s, not everyone could afford a ship to cruise the Mississippi River. Some folks had steamboats, and some folks had rafts. These water craft helped people transport goods for sale down to New Orleans. Then they would be shipped to the Atlantic Coast, South America, or Europe. You can build an edible raft!

Materials needed:
- Large pretzel rods
- Peanut butter
- Graham crackers
- Fruit roll-up (any flavor)
- Coffee stirrer, straw or popsicle stick

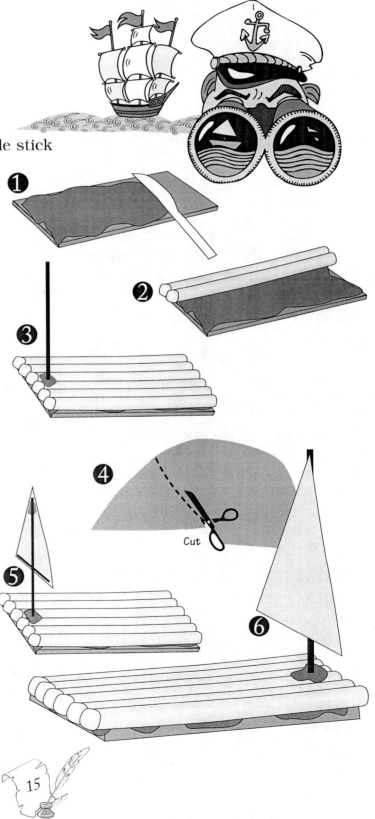

1 Spread a thick layer of peanut butter over two graham cracker sections. Set them close together.

2 Lay pretzel rods in a row on the graham cracker.

3 Use peanut butter to attach a standing mast on top of the raft. The mast can be a coffee stirrer, popsicle stick, straw, or whatever else.

4 Cut a triangular sail from a fruit roll-up, piece of cheese, or other light material. Use toothpicks to make it stick and stay flat.

5 Attach the sail to the top of the mast with peanut butter.

6 Float your raft to the table where you can eat it!

Cut

15

A Growing Nation

During the early 1800s, Americans had to make some tough decisions about the future of their country. The population was growing rapidly. The adventurous pioneers were getting restless. The United States needed to expand. But where?

The Louisiana Purchase of 1803 helped solve some of those problems. And it created some more. Now there was a whole new wilderness, complete with a foreign population, that the United States had to govern and control. But President Thomas Jefferson was ready to meet that challenge!

Answer the following math questions that people may have needed to solve during this era of change.

1 Louisiana became the 18th U.S. state on April 30, 1812. How many years after the Louisiana Purchase did Louisiana become a state? _____

2 The Louisiana Purchase covered approximately 827,000 square miles. How many square kilometers was this land? _____
(Hint: 1 sq. mi. = 2.59 sq. km.)

3 The total price of the Louisiana Purchase was $15 million dollars. Of that amount, $11,250,000 was paid directly. The United States agreed to pay for the rest by assuming French debts owned to American citizens. How much was that amount? _____

4 If you can grow 30 bushels of wheat on each acre of your Midwestern farm and your harvest totals 18,000 bushels of wheat, how many acres do you own?

_____

5 The Mississippi River begins in Lake Itasca, Minnesota and flows out to the Gulf of Mexico for 2,340 miles. How many 20-foot trees would equal 1 mile?

_____

(Hint: 1 mi. = 5.280 ft.)

6 The Louisiana Purchase didn't just add land to America. It attracted people. In 1790, the U.S. population totaled 3.9 million. In 1810, the population was 7.2 million. How many more people lived in the U.S. in 1810 than in 1790? _____

16

Rollin' On The River

President Thomas Jefferson's original instructions in 1803 to James Monroe and Robert Livingston were to purchase New Orleans and the Floridas from France. If the United States owned New Orleans, they could sail goods down the Mississippi River safely through Spanish territory. Then they could be shipped right out of the port city toward markets in Europe and along the Atlantic coast. The Mississippi River was a valuable trade route for the Americans, and they wanted to protect it.

We built a model of a riverboat to test the currents on the river. Look at the diagrams to answer the following questions.

1. Riverboat #1 is traveling in which direction? _____ the current

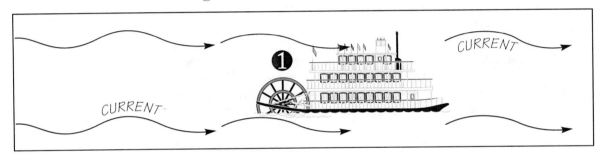

2. Riverboat #2 is traveling in which direction? _____ the current

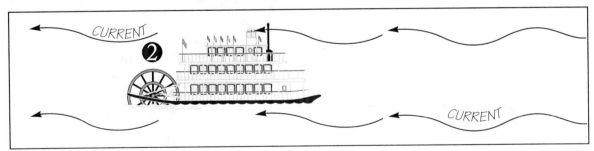

3. Riverboat #3 is traveling *with* the current, but at the same speed as the current, so it is moving at a total of _____ knots.

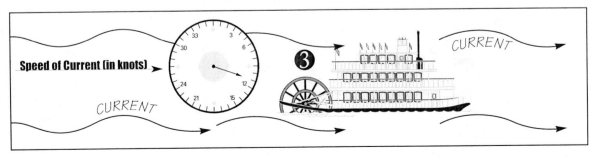

17

4. Riverboat #4 is traveling *against* the current. It is steaming hard at 18 knots. The riverboat is actually moving forward at _____ knots.

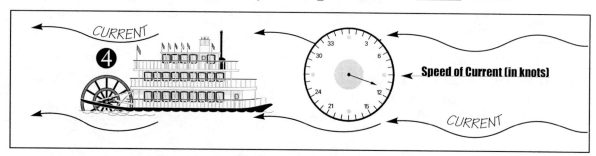

5. Riverboat #5 is coming in to dock and slows down 1 knot. Given the speed of the current, the riverboat's total forward speed is _____ knots.

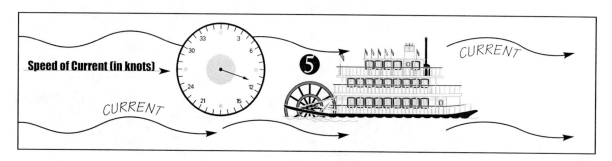

6. A horse is being ridden along the riverbank at the same speed as riverboat #5 is going while coming in to dock. To figure out how fast the horse is going, convert knots to miles per hour (you can use a calculator on this one!):

    _____ knots x 1.1516 = _____ miles per hour

    Hint: Round your numbers up!

18

Mississippi Mud Pie

A waitress named Jenny Meyer first named Mississippi Mud Pie when she moved to Vicksburg. A gooey chocolate pie that the cook whipped up reminded her of the mud-caked valley she saw right after the 1927 Mississippi River Flood. She said, "That reminds me of that Mississippi Mud!" And the name stuck (like mud). Make a Mississippi Mud Pie and celebrate American ownership of the Mississippi River, thanks to the Louisiana Purchase of 1803!

Mississippi Mud Pie

Ingredients

18 crushed chocolate cookies
3 tablespoons melted butter
1 large package instant chocolate pudding
cold milk (use amount from box's pie recipe)
chocolate sauce
1/2 cup nuts (almonds, pecans, or peanuts)
1/2 cup chocolate chips
whipped topping

Directions

Mix the crushed cookies and butter together.
Press the mixture into the bottom of a pie plate.
Chill for 30 minutes in the fridge. Prepare the
pudding according to the pie directions
on the box and pour it into the crust.
Drizzle chocolate sauce on the top.
Sprinkle with nuts and chocolate chips. Add
whipped topping to (where else?) the top!
Return the pie to the fridge and chill for
the time on the pudding box's pie
recipe. Then enjoy!

19

The Important Visitor

The Marquis de Lafayette was a French nobleman who helped the American colonists win the war for independence. In 1777, he and several other French army officers came to help fight (without pay). These Frenchmen were only a few of the many people who came from other countries to help the Americans during this rough time.

Lafayette was wounded at the Battle of Brandywine in 1777 and served with General George Washington at Valley Forge. In 1779, he traveled to France to seek aid for his American friends. He also helped enact the Treaty of Paris that ended the Revolutionary War in 1783.

In 1824, the Marquis de Lafayette came back to the United States for a visit. During his year-long tour of the country, Lafayette stopped in New Orleans for five days in April. He stayed in the Cabildo, which was the main state government building during that time.

The Sala Capitular, the very same room where the final transfers of the Louisiana Purchase took place in 1803, was completely redecorated just for Lafayette's visit! They got new furniture, wallpaper, draperies, carpets, wall hangings, and chandeliers. The Sala Capitular, formerly a courtroom, was turned into an elegant drawing room where Lafayette could meet and talk with important delegations of people.

Fast Fact

Lafayette's full name was Marie Joseph Paul Yves Roche Gilbert du Motier!

Read the information above and answer the following questions.

1. The Marquis de _____ was from _____.

2. New furnishings were installed in the _____ for Lafayette's important _____ to New Orleans.

3. During the war for independence, Lafayette was _____ at the Battle of _____

4. The _____ of Paris ended the _____ War in 1783.

5. Lafayette stayed in the _____, a state government building.

20

Different Folks

The Louisiana Territory presented an interesting challenge for the United States government. America was the land of the free, home of the immigrant. Now there were several more ethnic groups and races to govern in this new territory.

These new and different folks who lived in Louisiana included: Creoles (French and Spanish descent), Germans, English, Acadians, free blacks, Native Americans, and slaves. Then more American settlers migrated from Tennessee and Kentucky and all over the eastern states. Everyone had their own traditions, customs, and ways of living life. The groups needed to get along with each other in order to live in this new place peacefully.

What is your ethnic heritage? Share your diversity with other people by teaching them about it. Name one example from your ethnic heritage for every category below.

Holiday: _____

Food: _____

Religion: _____

Cool Place: _____

Historic Site: _____

Music: _____

Clothing: _____

Dance: _____

diverse: different or varied

ethnic: a group of people who have the same language, culture, or religion

custom: a way of doing something that has been accepted among a group of people

Sail Away!

People didn't have airplanes to fly during the 1800s. James Monroe and Robert Livingston had to cross the Atlantic Ocean on ships when they traveled to France. Build a ship of your own!

Materials needed:

- 2 clean milk cartons
- 2 straws
- playdough
- long piece of string or yarn
- brown and white construction paper
- scissors
- glue and tape
- one popsicle stick

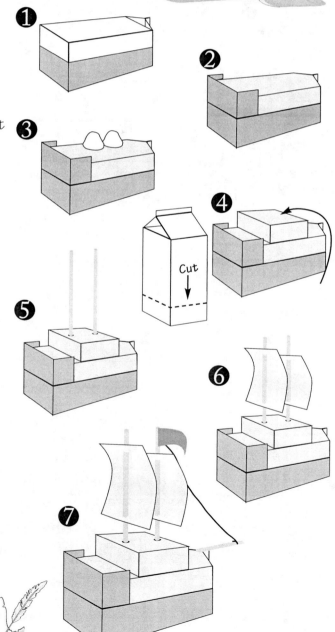

❶ Set the milk carton on its side. Cover the bottom half with brown paper (it may take two sheets).

❷ Cover the rest of the carton with white paper. Tape another piece of brown paper around the back of the carton. Leave one inch sticking up at the top, and go down 2 inches on either side.

❸ Roll two small hills of playdough and set them in the center of the ship.

❹ Cut the bottom section (3 inches up) off of the second milk carton. Turn the carton section so that the open part faces down and cover it with white paper. Tape the "ship deck" to the center of the ship directly over the playdough hills.

❺ Use a pencil to jab two holes into the deck right above each hill. Stick a straw "mast" through each hole into each hill.

❻ Cut a 3-inch square and a 4-inch square from white paper. Poke two holes in each and place these "sails" onto the masts.

❼ Cut a flag to glue at the top of one mast. Glue the popsicle stick straight out in front of the boat. Tie the string from the front mast to the stick. Decorate your boat with waves, a door, portholes, and whatever else you like!

22

Crops, Goods, Services, and Citizens

So why was that Louisiana territory so important to the United States? They didn't know it then, but we eventually gained 15 states from it! And those states all produce crops, goods, services, and hardworking citizens that are helping to build the American economy every day.

Match each delicious crop with the correct picture.

____ 1. Corn

____ 2. Sweet potatoes

____ 3. Rice

____ 4. Apples

____ 5. Barley

____ 6. Wheat

____ 7. Cheese

____ 8. Tomatoes

____ 9. Watermelon

____ 10. Pecans

a.

b.

c.

d.

e.

f.

g.

h.

i.

j.

23

Just Imagine . . .

Now that you have learned about some of the intense history surrounding the Louisiana Purchase, you can begin to imagine all of the "what if" scenarios. What would America look like today if France had decided not to sell the Louisiana Territory in 1803? Would New Orleans still be New Orleans? What would have happened if Britain or Spain had bought it? Would we be speaking Spanish right now? What if the American settlers and French citizens who were living in the territory decided to become their own country? Who knows what could have happened? History and geography could have been very different without this amazing transaction!

Draw America the way you think it would look like 50 years after 1803 if we never purchased the Louisiana Territory. Label countries, states, cities, and other important landmarks on your 1853 map.

Add Unto U.S.

The Louisiana Purchase sure didn't remain a big chunk of land for long because if there's one thing Americans know how to do, it's explore and settle. Before long, territories started cropping up everywhere. Towns and cities were being founded and new natural wonders were being discovered. One by one (and sometimes split into two!) the territories became states and began to help put together the America we live in today.

Label the states that were included (partially and fully) in the Louisiana Purchase. How many are there? Color them red. Color the western states blue. Color the eastern states green. Mark New Orleans with a star!

 "Never before had the world seen the kind of national expansion which gave our people all that part of the American continent lying west of the thirteen original States; the greatest landmark in which was the Louisiana Purchase."

– *President Theodore Roosevelt, 1903*
(from the Address at the Dedication Ceremonies of the Louisiana Purchase Exposition)

Louisiana Purchase Trivia!

Mark the trivia facts you believe are true!

TRUE / FALSE   France charged only four cents for each acre of Louisiana.

TRUE / FALSE   Baring & Company, a British bank, financed the Louisiana Purchase between the United States and France even though England was at war with France.

TRUE / FALSE   Louisiana Territory was more racially and ethnically diverse than any other region in the United States at the time.

TRUE / FALSE   French negotiators suggested $22.5 million at first, but James Monroe talked them down to $15 million (60 million francs).

TRUE / FALSE   There were three agreements to the Louisiana Purchase: a treaty of cession and two agreements to agree on how payment would occur.

TRUE / FALSE   President Thomas Jefferson was organizing an expedition, led by Meriwether Lewis and William Clark, to explore the Louisiana Territory even before the deal was made!

TRUE / FALSE   The U.S. Senate ratified the treaty with a vote of 24-7.

TRUE / FALSE   Many people said the purchase was not constitutional because the president wasn't specifically given power to buy land.

TRUE / FALSE   The Louisiana Purchase is the largest area of territory ever added to the United States at one time.

TRUE / FALSE   The Spanish only gave up physical possession of Louisiana to France on November 30, even though the U.S. had bought it months prior!

TRUE / FALSE   Louisiana was the first state carved from the Louisiana Purchase.

Urgent Telegram!

Most forms of communication that we use today weren't available during the early 1800s. There were no fax machines, email programs, telephones, or telegraphs. Sending letters through the post office was even slower than it is now. So what did people do when they needed to send an urgent message?

Paul Revere could dash off on a midnight horse ride, but negotiators James Monroe and Robert Livingston were all the way across the Atlantic Ocean in France! President Jefferson had secretly told them to spend more if they needed to, so the two men decided to use good judgement and make a decision on their own.

Napoleon made his incredible offer to sell the whole territory on April 11. Both sides agreed upon the $15 million price by late April, treaties were signed in May, and the United States didn't get the news until July 3!

What if James Monroe and Robert Livingston COULD have sent a telegram? In 50 words or less, write down what you think it would have said.

TELEGRAM

To: Thomas Jefferson
President of the United States

Date: _____

STOP _____

_____

_____

_____

_____

_____

_____

_____

STOP Respectfully yours, _____ STOP

27

Purchase Poem

What creative words can you think of to describe the events of the Louisiana Purchase? Think of the process to get the land, the people who lived there, and how the territory changed the United States.

Write your own poem about the Louisiana Purchase on the tablet below. Use any style.

28

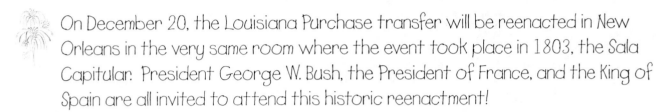

Celebrate the Louisiana Purchase Bicentennial!

On December 20, the Louisiana Purchase transfer will be reenacted in New Orleans in the very same room where the event took place in 1803, the Sala Capitular. President George W. Bush, the President of France, and the King of Spain are all invited to attend this historic reenactment!

The New Orleans Museum of Art will host an international exhibition of artifacts related to the Louisiana Purchase, including Napoleon's throne and Thomas Jefferson's easy chair, paintings, sculptures, historical documents, military artifacts, furniture, clothing, and more. The objects will come from famous museums around the world, including the Louvre, Versailles, Monticello, the National Gallery of Art, and others!

The New Orleans Botanical Garden will showcase an exhibit of plants and growing techniques inspired by the gardens at the Monticello home of Thomas Jefferson and at Chateau de Malmaison, the home of Napoleon!

The Louisiana Philharmonic Orchestra, Acadiana Symphony Orchestra of Lafayette, and New Orleans Opera Association will perform concerts (inspired by the Louisiana Purchase) in several Louisiana cities!

The Louisiana State Museum will present "One Nation Under God: The Church, the State, and the Louisiana Purchase" at the Cabildo in New Orleans.

Louisiana Purchase Bicentennial celebrations will take place across the country in states involved in this historic land deal that changed America!

29

Additional Resources to Explore!

BOOKS

The Louisiana Purchase: An American Story by John Churchill Chase & Emilie Dietrich Griffin

A Wilderness So Immense: The Louisiana Purchase and the Destiny of America by Jon Kukla

The Louisiana Purchase by Thomas Fleming

Mr. Jefferson's Lost Cause: Land, Farmers, Slavery, and the Louisiana Purchase
    by Roger G. Kennedy

Jefferson's Great Gamble: The Remarkable Story of Jefferson, Napoleon and the Men Behind the Louisiana Purchase by Charles A. Cerami

Lewis and Clark and the Louisiana Purchase 1803-1806 by Earl B. McElfresh

The Louisiana Purchase: An Encyclopedia by Junius P. Rodriguez

The Constitutional History of the Louisiana Purchase: 1803-1812 by Everett Somerville Brown

WEB SITES

http://lsm.crt.state.la.us/cabildo/cab4.htm

http://www.sec.state.la.us/purchase-index.htm

http://www.monticello.org/jefferson/lewisandclark/louisiana.html

http://www.archives.gov/exhibit_hall/american _originals

http://www.louisianahistoricalsociety.org

http://departments.mwc.edu/jmmu/louisiana_purchase/index.html

VIDEO

Louisiana Purchase (1941), starring Bob Hope

MAGAZINES

Travel America, March/April 2003

30

Glossary

aid: help given to someone else

ambitious: having a desire to achieve a particular goal

cede (renounce): to give up or give, usually by signing a treaty

delegation: a group of people chosen to represent others

folly: a lack of common sense or normal good judgement; a dumb idea

foreign: being from another country

national security: the safety of a nation

negotiate: to bargain for a deal that everyone can agree with

obstinate: stubborn

ratify: to formally approve and confirm

Answer Key

Page 8
L, L, U, L, L, U, U, L, U

Page 9
1. Cuba; 2. Cayman Islands; 3. Jamaica; 4. Haiti; 5. Guadeloupe; 6. Martinique; 7. Bahamas; 8. Turks & Caicos Islands; 9. Dominican Republic; 10. Puerto Rico

Page 10
Dress - $2.10; Hammer - $1.58; Cotton - $3.15; Nails - $1.05; Sugar - $1.84; Flour - $1.31

Page 13
a. France; b. England; c. Canada; d. Spain; e. Mexico; f. United States

Page 16
1. 9 years; 2. 2,141,930 square kilometers; 3. 3,750,000; 4. 600 acres 5. 264 trees 6. 3.3 million

Page 17
1. with; 2. against; 3. 22 knots; 4. 7 knots; 5. 12 knots; 6. 14 m.p.h.

Page 20
1. Lafayette, France; 2. Sala Capitular, visit; 3. Wounded; Brandywine; 4. Treaty, Revolutionary; 5. Cabildo

Page 23
1. i; 2. e; 3. a; 4. b; 5. h; 6. c; 7. g; 8. f; 9. d; 10. j

Page 26 They are all TRUE!

Index

Barbé-Marbois, François 11
bicentennial 29
Bonaparte, Napoleon 5, 8, 9, 10, 11, 27, 29
Cabildo 20
de Lafayette, Marquis 20
ethnic diversity 21, 26
France 5, 8, 9, 10, 11, 12, 14, 26, 27
Great Britain 9, 10, 11, 26
Guadeloupe 9
Jefferson, Thomas 5, 14, 16, 26, 27, 29
L'Ouverture, Toussaint 9

Lewis, Meriwether 26
limited government 8
Livingston, Robert 5, 11, 14, 22, 27
Louisiana 5, 9, 10, 11, 12, 16, 21, 25, 26, 29
Louisiana Purchase 5, 12, 13, 16, 24, 27, 29
Martinique 9
Mississippi River 10, 15, 16, 17, 19
Monroe, James 5, 11, 14, 22, 26, 27

New Orleans 5, 10, 12, 17, 20, 29
Sala Capitular 20, 29
slave revolt 9, 11
Spain 9, 10, 11
St. Domingue 9, 10, 11
trade 9, 10, 11, 15, 17, 23
United States 5, 10, 11, 12, 13, 16, 24, 25, 27
unlimited government 8
U.S. Constitution 5, 14, 26
West Indies 8, 9
William, Clark 26